Original title:
Lemon Tree Tales

Copyright © 2025 Creative Arts Management OÜ
All rights reserved.

Author: Julian Carmichael
ISBN HARDBACK: 978-1-80586-295-6
ISBN PAPERBACK: 978-1-80586-767-8

Tales of the Tangy Twilight

In a garden where the sun did gleam,
A feathered friend began to scheme.
He donned a hat and made a noise,
Chasing the shadows with his joys.

A swirl of zest upon the breeze,
With giggles that brought all to their knees.
The butterfly danced in a lemony sway,
As the fruit laughed out at the end of day.

Mellow Yellow Musings

A jester jumped on a fruity scene,
Wearing a shirt that was bright green.
With a bounce and a hop, he stole the show,
Tickling marigolds row by row.

He chuckled as he juggled some fruit,
Lemons rolling in an acrobatic route.
A giggle here, a giggle there,
Who knew a laugh grew in the air?

The Alchemy of Citrus

In a world where juice meets laughter,
A wizard laughed, chasing after.
He mixed a potion with a zesty twirl,
Turning sour into a sugary whirl.

With a sprinkle of jest and a twist of fate,
He brewed up magic that tasted great.
Banana smiled as the orange danced,
While the lime just giggled, completely entranced.

Sweet and Sour Reveries

In a dream where fruits begin to talk,
A tangerine did a silly walk.
It bumped into grapes, and oh, what fun,
Together they shined under the sun.

The kiwis chuckled, a fuzzy joke,
As apples blushed, beginning to choke.
In this orchard of quirks and mirth,
Every fruit found its place and worth.

Bitter and Sweet Confessions

In the garden where the fruit does glow,
A tale of tang and zest we know.
One bite brings laughter, another a wince,
In citrus chaos, we find our mints.

Life's a fruitcake, oddly stacked,
With twists of fate that leave us cracked.
The bitter bites, they chase the sweet,
In every slice, there's joy to meet.

Sun-Drenched Dreams

Underneath the blazing sun,
Zesty visions, oh what fun!
Juicy whispers in the breeze,
Citrus smiles bring us to ease.

Sipping sunshine, tasting light,
With every zest, we feel so bright.
Twisting tales, both rich and ripe,
In every sip, the joy is type.

The Citrus Serenade

A chorus sung by fruit on high,
With melodies that make us sigh.
Lemons, limes, a fruity band,
They play each note with zest so grand.

In every squeeze, a laugh takes flight,
A tangy twist, a pure delight.
Dance of flavors so absurd,
A serenade that's truly heard.

A Symphony of Slices

Chop and dice, the flavors blend,
A comedic dance that seems to bend.
Each bite a note, both sweet and sour,
In this ensemble, we find our power.

Juicy rhythms, a fruity spree,
A laugh-out-loud citrus jubilee.
With every slice, the fun unfolds,
A symphony that never grows old.

Harvesting Hope and Sunshine

In the garden, dreams abound, A yellow orb upon the ground. I twist and squeeze, what do I find? A beverage for the thirsty mind!

Beneath the sunlight's playful glare, I dance with joy, no hint of care. The fruits of labor, sweet and bright, Each citrus grin is pure delight!

My neighbors peek, with jealous eyes, A zesty world, where laughter flies. With every squeeze, a giggle grows, As lemonade flows, and chaos flows!

Oh, what a sight, the juice it spills, A splash of joy, and grandest thrills. In every cup, a story spark, Harvesting hope, brightening dark!

Citrus Blossoms in the Breeze

Whispers of spring, as blooms appear, With petals soft, and scents so clear. Bees buzz around, in happy haste, A citrus riot, none to waste!

Each blossom holds a silly jest, A tipple sweet, the very best. I twirl and spin amidst the bloom, In this sweet chaos, laughter looms!

For every bud that blooms anew, A chuckle, giggle, and maybe two. The sunbeams play their funny tricks, As I dodge the bees, the pollen flicks!

In the breeze, such tales unfold, Of fruity dreams and laughter bold. With citrus cheer, I'll raise a toast, To breezy days I love the most!

Echoes of Fruitful Days

In the grove where shadows dance, I hear the echoes of chance. Each juicy morsel tells a tale, Of silly pranks and endless hail!

A squirt of juice, a playful fling, The dogs all bark, the children sing. Each fruit a treasure, bright and bold, With stories of the weeks of old!

I toss a rind, it sails so free, And hit the cat, oh what a spree! It leaps and bounds, all in a twist, My citrus pranks are hard to resist!

At twilight's call, we gather round, With joyful hearts, our laughter's found. These fruitful days, forever stay, With echoes of joy, come what may!

Revelations Beneath the Boughs

Underneath the leafy shroud, I hear the laughter, warm and loud. A quirky quest for fruit so fine, The secrets hide, the sun must shine!

Each tangy burst brings giggles near, The neighbors come with zest and cheer. A secret stash, a tangy find, Where silly tales are left behind!

In shadows cool, the crew convenes, With fruit-shaped hats and silly schemes. We plot and plan a fruity feast, With punchlines flying, laughter increased!

The boughs above, they sway and bow, To all our antics, here and now. With every sip, a grinning face, Revelations found in this fruity place!

Harvest of Light

In a sunny patch, I found some fruit,
A citrus flair, oh what a hoot!
With a twist and a turn, they slipped and rolled,
Their shiny yellow skins, a sight to behold.

I grabbed one quick, it bounced away,
Like a little sunbeam wanting to play!
It laughed at me, then claimed the breeze,
Dancing along, oh, such a tease!

I chased it down, my silly quest,
Feeling like a fool, but I confess,
The joy it brought, oh what a shock,
A tree full of giggles, a citrus clock!

Finally caught, it gave a squeeze,
Sprayed zest in my face, oh what a tease!
With every drop, laughter spread bright,
In a harvest of glow, pure delight.

Under the Citrus Sky

Out in the orchard, the sun shining high,
A lemon so bold, it caught my eye.
With a flick of its stem, it waved hello,
I chuckled and thought, what a funny show!

The branches danced, like a wild parade,
Lemons in hats, oh the jokes they made!
One lemon quipped, with a cheeky grin,
'Life's a zest fest, come join the spin!'

I stood there laughing, the scene quite grand,
Fruity jesters across the land.
A squeeze of fun in every bite,
Beneath the citrus sky, oh such delight!

Together we danced, leaves rustled with glee,
In this sunny spot, forever carefree.
Lemon laughter echoing, fading away,
Under the citrus sky, I chose to stay.

When Life Gives You Zest

When life hands you fruit, don't make a frown,
One bite of zest, you'll never drown!
I took a big plunge, oh what a thrill,
My taste buds giggled, a citrus spill!

A lemon joked, 'Don't you fret,
I'm here for laughter, a sour duet!'
With a twist of my face, I wore a grin,
Each puckering taste made me laugh within.

Rolling along, they tumbled right by,
Citrus comedy, oh me, oh my!
They bounced and they spun, full of cheer,
In every drop, a little joke clear!

So when life gives you zest, take a bite,
Dance with the flavors, feel the delight!
For in every sour, there's sweetness entwined,
A harvest of humor, life redefined.

Stories from the Sun-Kissed Orchard

In a sun-kissed orchard, tales come alive,
Lemon-shaped stories that thrive and survive.
With peels full of laughter, they share with glee,
Each twist and each turn, pure jubilee!

A wise old fruit said, 'Listened here, mate,
Life's like a lemon, don't call it fate!
Just sprinkle some sugar, make it anew,
Turn sour to sweet, dance in the dew!'

I perched on a branch, took in the sound,
Fruits chirping slyly, a happy-go-round.
With every bright tale, they wobbled and swayed,
In this orchard of laughter, worries allayed.

So gather 'round folks, for the stories are sweet,
In this sun-kissed realm, where laughter's the treat.
With lemonade dreams, we'll sip and we'll toast,
To the tales of the orchard, we cherish the most!

Golden Fruits

Under the sun, they shine so bright,
Yellow orbs, a hilarious sight.
Squirrels argue, who claims the best?
In this orchard, there's never a rest.

With laughter bubbling, we climb so high,
Wobbling branches, we reach for the sky.
A juicy drop lands on my head,
Now I'm a clown, with zest widespread!

Sunshine giggles in every slice,
Fruits of joy, a majestic paradise.
Jokes and smiles, they'll never stop,
As the sun dips low, we shout, "Don't drop!"

In the frenzy, we dance and sway,
Golden fruits lead the fun ballet.
With every bite, we chuckle and cheer,
Creating memories that linger near.

Golden Memories

Remember the time, the fruit fight begun?
Laughter erupted, oh, what fun!
Splattered zest on our shirt and hair,
Sticky sweet, not a single care.

We made crowns from the leaves we stole,
Adventurers brave, we played our role.
With every swing and every twist,
Golden moments, impossible to resist.

A treasure hunt, oh what a spree,
Chasing shadows, wild as can be.
Every corner hid a funny prank,
With giggles echoing, we gave thanks.

When day turned to dusk, tales spun around,
Silly stories in every sound.
Time in the orchard, where laughter roams,
Golden memories crafted, like sweet poems.

Tales from the Zesty Canopy

In the leafy realm, up high and free,
Silly critters play hide and seek with glee.
Birds chuckle loudly at our clumsy feet,
Oh, the joy of citrusy retreat!

Each branch a tale, every leaf a grin,
With tangy giggles that come from within.
A band of friends, in zesty delight,
Chasing shadows until the night.

A squirrel in sunglasses, looking so grand,
Feels like royalty in this playful land.
With wit and whimsy, we gather the fun,
Under the canopy, our laughter's in the sun.

Slipping and sliding, we take a chance,
With zesty dreams, we laugh and dance.
In each twist of fate, the stories unfold,
In this funny orchard, the tales are bold.

The Whispering Citrus Leaves

The leaves are laughing, can you hear?
Whispers of joy, far and near.
Tickling ears with fun surprise,
Secrets of citrus beneath bright skies.

As the wind sings tunes, we follow along,
Swinging and twirling, we can't go wrong.
Sneaky squirrels join in the jest,
Bouncing about, oh, the zest fest!

Each rustle brings a goofy grin,
In this lively dance, we all fit in.
A spritz of juice, down the slide,
Who knew fruit could be such fun to ride?

Through laughter and games in a citrus spree,
The whispering leaves share joy so free.
So clap your hands, let the laughter flow,
In this merry grove, we always glow.

Fragrant Shadows

In the afternoon light, the shadows play,
Popping out tricks in a humorous way.
With orange peels as our joyful hats,
We're kings and queens of the citrus flats!

Under the canopy, we share our glee,
Creating stories as zesty as can be.
A fruit juggling act, watch out! Oh dear!
A citrus cascade, oh so near!

Listen closely to the giggles abound,
As fragrant shadows dance all around.
With each chuckle, the sun grows tired,
In this playful realm, we're all inspired.

So let the laughter dip and weave,
In this garden, we choose to believe.
Fragrant shadows, with joy we play,
In our funny land, there'll always stay.

Reflections in a Citrus Well

In a well of bright yellow fruit,
I found a laugh that can't be mute.
A squirrel danced with great delight,
Chasing shadows, what a sight!

Beneath the sun, the warmth was grand,
A wobbly chair, I tried to stand.
I slipped and fell, oh what a scene,
With citrus juice, I looked like a queen!

The neighbors peered, their faces grinned,
While I, with zest, felt like a win.
I tossed a slice, it flew with flair,
And landed right in someone's hair!

A giggly crowd began to grow,
With lemonade jokes, the laughter flowed.
In this citrus world so bright and bold,
Every story is worth its gold!

Spheres of Lifelong Citrus Memories

A citrus ball rolled on the ground,
Chasing laughter, making sound.
With each bounce, it sparked a grin,
Like playful whispers on the skin.

Old friends gathered for a feast,
Joking 'bout the juice at least.
A pie so tart, it made us squeal,
As tongues twisted in a zestful reel.

An orange cat jumped in the fray,
Stealing snacks till the end of the day.
With each story shared and told,
Our memories shimmered, bright and bold.

A citrus hug, so warm and sweet,
With every bite, we savored the treat.
In every laugh, a world we'd find,
Lifelong joys, forever entwined!

The Honeyed Heart of Sunshine

Sunshine giggled, dressed in gold,
With sticky fingers, we were sold.
Dripping honey on our bread,
We danced around, our faces red.

A buzzing bee, a friend so near,
Joined our fun without a fear.
We shared our charms, we shared our glee,
As sugary drips dripped down a tree!

Oh, what a jam, a honeyed mess,
With citrus tunes, we felt so blessed.
Skateboards flew; laughter roamed wide,
In this sun, we surely abide.

We mixed and stirred, oh what a sight,
Tasting joy till the fall of night.
In every giggle, the world aligned,
With honeyed hearts forever entwined!

Secrets Drenched in Citrus Glow

Beneath the glow of citrus bright,
Secrets danced like stars at night.
A prankster orange, sly and wise,
Sprayed juice right into our eyes!

Giggling friends, we plotted schemes,
To squeeze the zest from all our dreams.
In the twilight, tricks would fly,
Underneath the joyous sky.

A hidden stash of candies near,
Each bite burst forth with citrus cheer.
As shadows grew, we claimed our space,
With fruity bursts, we'd laugh and race!

Secrets lingered, sweet and bright,
Carved with giggles through the night.
In every zesty, secret glow,
Our playful spirits began to grow!

Tangy Memories

In a garden of zest, so sweet and bright,
A squirrel stole fruit, oh what a sight!
He wobbled and danced, ran fast and free,
Chased by the neighbor's old cat, oh me!

With every twist, a laugh was shared,
Bouncing around, as if they dared.
The fruit took flight, in the summer breeze,
They tumbled and rolled, with such silly ease.

Jars of sunshine, we'd make each day,
Sipping on happiness, in a funny way.
With a twist of a joke, and a pinch of cheer,
Our tangy memories, forever near.

Each taste a giggle, each sip a smile,
Funny little tales that go on for miles.
So here's to the zest, and all the humor,
In the swirl of the sweet, we find our rumor.

The Color of Brightness

Mornings painted in shades of cheer,
The sun comes up, it's time for beer!
But not the kind that leaves us sore,
A fizzy lemon drink, we'll all adore.

A splash of yellow, vibrant and bold,
With a twist of laughter, as stories unfold.
The neighbors come by, with their curious grins,
As they sip from cups, where the funny begins.

We toast to the chaos, to joy without end,
As the bubbles tickle and laughter bends.
Every sip a tale, bursting with flair,
In these bright moments, we haven't a care.

Wrapped in the sunshine, we giggle aloud,
Living each moment, oh aren't we proud?
In the color of brightness, we find our tune,
With laughter and love, under the moon.

Branches and Blossoms

Under branches thick, where the laughter grows,
We picked some fruits, all in a row.
Slipping and sliding, we danced through the leaves,
With giggles and grins, oh who'd believe?

The blossoms were wild, with colors that shone,
Petals like confetti, our laughter alone.
As bees buzzed nearby, we started a game,
Swapping our stories, but who's to blame?

We made syrup from smiles, a sticky delight,
And shared silly secrets on that sunny night.
Branches swayed low, as the wind joined in,
In the midst of the fun, happiness would win.

With each little hop, and each fruit-packed cheer,
Life tasted sweeter when friends were near.
So here's to the moments, so funny and free,
In the branches and blossoms, forever we'll be.

Revelations in Yellow

In kitchens that sparkle, with hints of sun,
We tossed in our laughter, oh wasn't it fun?
With zest in the air, and stories to tell,
Each slice was a joke, each laugh rang a bell.

The yellow fruit whispered its juicy delight,
As we whipped up mishaps that felt just right.
A splash of sweet syrup, a curl of a peel,
In those light-hearted moments, we'd twist and we'd wheel.

We gathered around, friends both old and new,
With recipes written in giggles and stew.
A dash of confusion, a sprinkle of mirth,
In the sweetness of life, we found our true worth.

So here's to our revelations, bright as the sun,
In the funny little moments, we've all had our fun.
With joy in our hearts, and a twinkle of glee,
We cherish each laugh, as wild as can be.

The Sweet Tangle of Twisting Vines

In the garden, vines do twirl,
Like dancers in a merry whirl.
Fruit hangs low, so ripe and bright,
A citrus treasure, such delight.

The critters laugh, they prance around,
In this realm where joy is found.
But watch your step, or you might trip,
On wayward roots that dare to grip.

A squirrel tries to make a claim,
On a fruit that bears his name.
With a wink, he steals a bite,
And scampers off in pure delight.

With every twist, the laughter grows,
As nature plays, and mischief flows.
In this tangle, life's a game,
Yet every player's just the same.

A Child's Adventure in Citrus Land

A child awakes with visions bright,
Of oranges dancing in the light.
He ventures forth, with a grin so wide,
To explore the grove where wonders hide.

In Citrus Land, the trees all sway,
With golden fruit that shouts, 'Come play!'
He leaps and bounds, with glee unbound,
Each treasure found, a joy profound.

Suddenly comes a zesty squirt,
A sneaky lemon, oh what a flirt!
With laughter gushing from his lips,
He dodges droplets with acrobatic flips.

And as the sun begins to set,
He clutches fruits he'll not forget.
Home he goes, with tales to spin,
Of Citrus Land, where fun begins.

Breathing Life into Nature's Palette

In a garden painted bright and bold,
Nature's story quietly unfolds.
Each hue a burst, each scent a tease,
With citrus whispers in the breeze.

The oranges laugh, the limes they sing,
In this realm of zesty spring.
A butterfly flits, adorned in gold,
While secret flavors dare be told.

In every corner, colors blend,
A joyful chaos that won't end.
With each new bloom, the laughter grows,
As life rejoices in all it knows.

And when the sun dips low and deep,
The orchard sighs, then falls to sleep.
Yet in the dreams of night's embrace,
The magic lingers, full of grace.

Soft Rain on Golden Skins

It starts as a sprinkle, a gentle tease,
Soft rain falling like sweet melodies.
The fruit outside begins to gleam,
As nature dances in a dreamy dream.

Each drop a giggle, a playful sigh,
Caressing skins beneath the sky.
The trees all grin, their branches sway,
In this joyful, citrus ballet.

With puddles forming around their feet,
The world tastes better—it's all so sweet.
And kids in boots, splashing away,
Bring laughter to this rainy day.

So let the rain come, let it pour,
In this sun-filled place, who could ask for more?
For when the clouds finally take their flight,
The golden skins will shine so bright.

Embracing the Scent of Nostalgia

In the garden where laughter blooms,
The fruits carry whispers of youthful tunes.
With juicy bites, we smile and sigh,
Each zingy taste takes us back to July.

A splash of sunlight, a dash of fun,
We joke of the time when we out ran the sun.
With each tangy slice, we giggle and tease,
As we plot to squeeze joy from life's sweet squeeze.

Beneath the shade of a zesty brew,
The memories swirl like a sweet fondue.
We laugh at ourselves, we're silly, sincere,
Sharing our tales with a bubbly cheer.

So let us embrace this peeling delight,
With quirky tales that last through the night.
We'll dance with the zest, let our stories flow,
In a citrusy world where laughs always grow.

Harvesting the Sweets of Memory

In a grove where the laughter spills,
We gather the giggles, oh what a thrill!
Each fruit is a story, ripe on the vine,
Sweet memories linger, tasting divine.

With baskets in hand, we skip and we hop,
Collecting the moments that never will stop.
A roof made of leaves, a sky painted bright,
We savor the sweetness, oh what a sight!

We reminisce tales of mischief and fun,
Like the time grandpa painted the dog like the sun.
Juicy reflections of days far and near,
The fruits of our laughter, how sweet they appear.

So here's to the harvest, the laughs yet to sow,
In a world full of colors, let memories glow.
With each playful bite, our stories will twine,
Celebrating a past as zesty as wine.

Beneath the Zesty Canopy

Underneath the fan of bright yellow leaves,
We find our laughter in the rustling eves.
With citrusy smiles, our schemes start to spin,
As zany adventures invite us to grin.

The fruit is a jester, so plump and so round,
Each bite brings a chuckle, a joy to be found.
With friends right beside us, we share and we tease,
In this zesty haven, our troubles all freeze.

We swing from the branches, with giggles high-pitched,
Pretending to be monkeys, our silliness enriched.
The funny old sayings that make us all snort,
In this canopy of joy, laughter's the sport.

So let the sun sparkle, let the breezes play,
As we celebrate memories in our zany way.
Under leafy laughter, we find our sweet glee,
In this citrus kingdom, forever we're free.

A Dance with Citrus Colors

In a world where oranges cha-cha with lime,
We sway with the fruits and dance to the rhyme.
With giggly tunes that bounce all around,
Our feet feel the flavor of joy that we've found.

Each fruit has a flavor, so vibrant and bold,
Like stories of mischief, forever retold.
We stumble and twirl, and the laughter explodes,
As we find hidden treasures in our citrus abode.

A jig with the grapefruits, a twirl with the zest,
The joy of our childhood carved deep in our chest.
From pink juiced delights to yellows that glow,
In this fruity fiesta, our happiness flows.

So let's raise a glass, let's toast to the fun,
With a zest for adventure, our memories spun.
In this dance of delight, with colors so bright,
We'll savor the laughter that turns day to night.

Boughs That Hold the World

In a garden where the laughter grows,
Boughs hang low with juicy prose.
Each fruit a tale of silly sights,
Bouncing dreams in sunny flights.

A wizard with a zestful grin,
Crafts concoctions where smiles begin.
With every squeeze, the giggles pour,
In citrus lands, who could want more?

Juggling fruit on a wobbly chair,
Falling down without a care.
Orange peels for a quick surprise,
Laughter dances before our eyes.

As shadows stretch with the setting sun,
Everyone joins in the fruity fun.
Boughs that hold the world, so bright,
In each bite, we find delight.

Sipping Summer from a Citrus Glass

A pitcher filled with golden cheer,
Summer sips, the fun is near.
Tangy twists and frothy foam,
In this glass, we find our home.

With straw hats perched atop our heads,
We stir up jokes like silly threads.
Each slurp a giggle, a fruity jest,
Sipping joy, we're truly blessed.

The sun winks down, a playful tease,
As laughter drips like warm, sweet breeze.
Lemon slices bright and bold,
Sweetened memories begin to unfold.

In this glass, the world feels right,
Citrus laughter takes its flight.
Sipping summer, oh what a blast,
We toast to fun, let worries pass!

Essays of a Citrus Heart

With pages yellow, stories flow,
Essays penned with zest and glow.
About the peels and pithy fights,
Citrus hearts in silly flights.

The writer scribbles with a grin,
Each word a splash, let chaos begin.
Tales of fruit that spin and whirl,
In these essays, laughter twirls.

From orchard dreams to kitchen schemes,
Juicy plots burst at the seams.
Readers chuckle at every line,
In the citrus heart, all is fine.

Flip the pages, feel the fun,
Under the rays, we each have won.
Essays that tickle, oh, what a start,
In every word, beats a citrus heart.

Basking in Citrus Sunshine

Under the glow of a sunny tree,
We bask in smiles, so wild and free.
Citrus rays dance on our skin,
Moments bright as the fun begins.

A picnic spread with zest galore,
Laughter spills on the grassy floor.
With fruit hats stacked, we strut around,
In this sunshine, joy is found.

Squeezing lemons, making pies,
Turning frowns into surprise highs.
Jokes on tongues, with sticky hands,
In this world of sunny strands.

As day turns to night in its mellow glow,
We gather tales, let the laughter flow.
Basking in sunshine, we feel alive,
In citrus joy, we all thrive.

Citrus Serenade at Dusk

In the garden where the zesters play,
A tangy tune begins the day.
With citrus dreams and laughter bright,
The sun dips low, a merry sight.

A squirrel swings on branches high,
While lemon drops fall from the sky.
In every sip of zesty cheer,
We find our joy, the end is near.

Bumblebees dance with a silly twirl,
Chasing hues of a golden swirl.
Giggling fruits in a sleepy haze,
A citrus party, no time to laze!

Lemons grin from every nook,
Winking jokes like a funny book.
As the stars appear, we'll toast anew,
To citrus fun, and the crazy crew!

Fruits of Sunshine and Mirth

In a bowl of sunshine, bright and round,
A jester's jive can be found.
Citrus giggles, tangy and sweet,
Ready to dance on your next treat.

A fruit parade marches by,
With silly hats and an eye for pie.
Lime leaps high with a zesty cheer,
While oranges roll, spreading good cheer.

Pineapples wear fuzzy little shoes,
While grapefruits sing, spreading the news.
A chorus of flavors, all in line,
In this funny feast, the fruits all shine.

When the sun sets, we won't be done,
With citrus laughter, we've just begun.
Raise your glass to this fruity glee,
In the land of sunshine, we're wild and free!

Blossoms of Yesteryear in Bright Yellow

Once upon a time in orchards wide,
A band of yellow, nothing to hide.
With petals of laughter, they spun around,
In the warm breeze, their joy was found.

Chasing memories of days gone past,
A cackling crew, making moments last.
Fruits of splendor, ripe on the line,
Sharing their secrets, one zest at a time.

The flowers blush in the golden light,
Becoming jesters in the gentle night.
As fireflies flicker, they join the spree,
In this blooming show, find all the glee!

So raise your voice, let the laughter ring,
For in every petal, the joy they'll bring.
With chuckles and cheer, the blossoms play,
In a yellow fest, we'll dance all day!

Secrets of the Golden Grove

In a grove where fruits do play,
Orange giggles start the day.
Lemons dance in sunlit beams,
Mischief packs their juicy dreams.

A squirrel steals a ripe delight,
Chasing shadows, quick as light.
Bumbling bees with zestful hum,
Join the circus, round they run.

Golden Citrus Whispers

Whispers slip on peels so bright,
Chattering fruits in sheer delight.
Grapefruits gossip, oranges cheer,
In their orchard, laughter's near.

A parrot squawks a fruity tune,
Citrus hats beneath the moon.
Limes pull pranks on passerby,
With zesty jokes that never die.

Sun-Kissed Memories of Citrus

Sun-kissed moments, sweet and fun,
Every citrus is a pun.
A tangerine slips on a peel,
Grinning wildly, what a deal!

Frogs in hats with zestful glee,
Hopping 'round the citrus spree.
Tasting juice and catching rays,
Sipping giggles through the days.

The Sweetness in Every Zest

In each zest, a joke is spun,
Limes in limelight, having fun.
Oranges wear their sunny hats,
Making waves with citrus chats.

With every squeeze, laughter flies,
A fruity quarrel in disguise.
Sour faces turn to glee,
In this grove so wild and free.

Whispers in the Citrus Grove

Beneath the branches, secrets sway,
Where squirrels plot and children play.
A lemon dropped, and laughter flew,
As juice spilled out—what a view!

With citrus dreams and zesty schemes,
They dance around in sunlit beams.
A twist of fate, a citrus zest,
Oh, life is funny, we're truly blessed!

Whispers rustle, the lemons grin,
A splash of juice, let the fun begin!
A silly story that never grows old,
In yellow hues, a joy to behold.

So gather 'round, both young and spry,
As nature's jesters pass us by.
With every giggle, and every cheer,
In this grove, we shed a tear!

Crescendo of Citrus and Sky

In the grove, the sun shines bright,
Lemons laugh, oh what a sight!
A bird on a branch sings a tune,
As bees buzz in a citrus swoon.

A juggling act with fruit in hand,
Gives rise to chaos, oh so grand!
A slip, a trip, and everyone roars,
Life's citrusy joys, who could ask for more?

With rolling laughter and zest in the air,
The sky above is filled with flair.
From tart to sweet, oh what a mix,
In this fun melody, we play our tricks.

So raise your glass, let's toast tonight,
To all things zesty, funny, and bright!
In citrus harmony, we sway and spin,
In this joyful jest, let the fun begin!

The Laughter of Bright Yellow Days

Among the branches, bright and bold,
Stories of laughter, forever told.
With every lemon that's sliced in two,
A giggle escapes, how funny it grew.

Let's paint the town in shades of gold,
With zestful tales that never get old.
A mishap here, and a tumble there,
Through citrus chaos, we dance with flair.

Lemonade stands with faces so sweet,
A splash of humor, a zesty treat.
On sunny days, where joy appears,
We toast our laughter, shedding sweet tears.

So gather around, let's take a sip,
As life keeps giving this zesty trip.
In bright yellow days, together we play,
And laugh through life, come what may!

Stories of Bitter and Sweet

In a grove where flavors collide,
Stories of sweetness and tang abide.
A little mishap, a sour face,
Turns into laughter, an embrace of grace.

The fruit falls down with a plump little thud,
A splash of juice, oh what a flood!
With giggles echoing through the green,
In this citrus haven, we find the scene.

Life's juicy moments, both sharp and round,
In every giggle, a joy is found.
From sweet surprises to zesty dreams,
We laugh together, or so it seems.

So let's celebrate those moments dear,
In a grove of laughter, bring on the cheer!
With every slice, life's flavors we greet,
In stories of bitter, we find life sweet!

Sheltered Moments in Fragrant Glades

In the shade we plot and scheme,
Lemon drops like a sweet dream.
Laughter peels from sunlit leaves,
While dancing shadows play like thieves.

A squirrel steals a zesty treat,
With tiny feet, he skips, so fleet.
We giggle as he makes his dash,
His citrus heist, a comical splash.

In the breeze, jokes softly sway,
The sun and fruit lead us astray.
Before we know, the hour's gone,
We'll steal a slice and carry on.

So, gather round for tales we share,
In this grove, laughter fills the air.
With every quirk of nature's grace,
We find our joy in this bright space.

Citrus Chronicles of Memory

Once upon a fruity day,
We stumbled on a peppy play.
Squirrels conspired, birds did sing,
A citrus saga, oh what a fling!

With every squirt, a grin unleashed,
From laughter's bite, our cares were ceased.
The zest of life in every jest,
In foolish rinds, we find our best.

Beneath the boughs, the stories grow,
Of playful fights with juice in tow.
We chase the giggles, catch the sun,
In citrus lands where we have fun.

Back in time, with zestful cheer,
We crunch on tales that start right here.
In every twist, a hint of glee,
Our citrus tales forever free.

Picking Joy Among the Branches

We gather round, the fruit's in sight,
With bags to fill, we feel delight.
The branches sway with each big laugh,
As we seek luck on our citrus path.

A witty bird, he calls our name,
As if he knows our citrus game.
We race to snatch the juiciest prize,
With every peel, we share surprise.

The sun dips low, the day unwinds,
With sticky fingers, we realize,
These moments weave a joyful spree,
In every bite, our hearts feel free.

At twilight's call, we dance and cheer,
For fruit-laden joys, we hold so dear.
With tales of zest, we end the quest,
In citrus groves, we find our best.

Wild Dreams in Citrus Fields

In fields of gold where giggles sprout,
We dream of fruit, we leap about.
The scents of citrus fill the air,
As wild ideas dance without a care.

A band of bugs starts quite the show,
With fancy moves, they steal the glow.
Each little hop, a burst of cheer,
In this zany world, we've got no fear.

We chase the sun till shadows flee,
In wild passion, we feel so free.
With every twist of fate, we play,
And craft our dreams in citrus sway.

So, join us for a slice of glee,
In fields where laughter's meant to be.
With every laugh and joyful scream,
We soak in wild and zesty dreams.

A Symphony of Citrus Hues

In a garden bright and sunny,
Where shadows dance, oh so funny,
A yellow burst with bumpy skin,
Sings of joy, let the fun begin!

Butterflies twirl in happy flight,
While squirrels plot with all their might,
The branches sway, like a big band,
Playing tunes in the citrus land.

Jokes are made of sour and sweet,
As critters gather for a treat,
Lemons rolling, laughter gleams,
In this zesty world of dreams.

So come join the citrus parade,
With giggles spilled, no plans delayed,
In colors bright, let's have a blast,
With citrus hues that forever last!

The Lilt of Lemonade Languor

A glass of yellow, oh what cheer,
With ice cubes swimming, oh so dear,
Add sugar in a generous heap,
Sip and savor, no need for sleep!

The sun shines bright, a jolly tease,
While bees buzz by with utmost ease,
In shorts and hats, we lounge and grin,
In the lemonade world, we always win!

A splash of fun with lemon zest,
With every sip, we feel so blessed,
Splash fights start with laughter loud,
As we frolic, we're citrus proud!

So raise your glass, let's make a toast,
To lazy days we love the most,
With laughter sweet and tangy cheer,
In our lemonade dreams, we persevere!

Secrets Shared in Lemon Light

Under leaves that softly glow,
Whispers fly where breezes blow,
A fruity tale of giggles shared,
In lemon light, we are all dared.

Gossips float on a citrus breeze,
Where fairies hide behind the trees,
A secret spot, so sweetly bright,
Laughter sparkles, pure delight!

With a squirt that makes us glee,
Comes a smile as wide as the sea,
In lemon patches, fun abounds,
A world of joy, where laughter sounds.

So gather 'round, my playful friends,
In chat and chuckles, time transcends,
In the light of tangy sun,
Our silly secrets weave as one!

Sunlight's Embrace on Citrus Leaves

With rays of gold upon the trees,
The sunlight hugs with gentle ease,
Leaves shimmer bright, a dance affair,
A joyful moment, no care to spare!

Tiny critters find their groove,
In a citrus waltz, they sway and move,
Chasing shadows, laughing loud,
In this bright world, they're feeling proud!

Sunlight twinkles on fruit so round,
With every bounce, more joy is found,
In the embrace of warmth and cheer,
Every giggle, crystal clear!

So come, partake in nature's joke,
With sunshine's touch, let spirit soak,
In this billion-watt delight,
Life's a party, forever bright!

The Poetry of Citrus Pulp

In a grove of gleeful glee,
Citrus fruits dance with such glee.
Oranges giggle in the sun,
While grapefruits join in the fun.

Lemon's zest creates a cheer,
With every squirt, they draw near.
They tease the bees, all in a rush,
As laughter fills the sunny hush.

A tangerine spins on a branch,
Holding court, it takes a chance.
"Come one, come all, join my game!"
While cherries watch and hold their fame.

Then a pomegranate, bold and bright,
Claims it's the best, much to their fright.
Yet all agree, in their bold tone,
That fruit's a fruit, and never alone.

Vignettes Under the Golden Canopy

Beneath the sun's warm golden glow,
Citrus antics steal the show.
Limes roll 'round with cheeky glee,
While all the birds sing joyfully.

Twirling, dancing, ripe and round,
Grapefruits grin from ground to ground.
Their laughter echoes through the trees,
While pickles plot with a teasing breeze.

A monkey swings, oh what a sight!
He's trading jokes with orange light.
Juicy puns bounce with delight,
As lemons giggle day and night.

Under the canopy, joy abounds,
With every fruit, laughter resounds.
To harvest smiles in this sunny land,
Is what makes life quite so grand!

Whispering Spirits of the Orchard

In the orchard where spirits play,
Citrus laughs light up the day.
A whisper here, a giggle there,
Fruitful fun is everywhere.

Lemon fairies sing and sway,
Making mischief on display.
Beneath the leaves, they craft a plan,
For jesters in a fruit-filled clan.

Grapes in clusters form a band,
With berries dancing hand in hand.
Jokes are shared, and laughter flows,
As citrus magic brightly glows.

Peeling laughter from the rind,
Hidden treasures there to find.
With juicy tales told under bough,
We join the merriment here and now.

Echoes of Citrus Seasons

Through echoes bright of citrus cheer,
Summer laughter draws us near.
Oranges roll down hills so steep,
In races where the giggles leap.

Winter brings a zesty twist,
With funny frost, it can't be missed.
Snowmen made of fruits so bold,
Share tales of tropics, warm and gold.

Springtime blooms with citrus green,
The orchard's life is like a dream.
As blossoms burst, the fruits unite,
To play in sunlight, a joyous sight.

Autumn falls with ripe delight,
While liming spirits take to flight.
Through every season, fun resides,
In every slice, the laughter hides.

Zestful Whispers

In the garden of mirth, laughter grows,
Silly squirrels tell tales that nobody knows.
A sprite in the leaves starts a comedic show,
While the shadows of citrus dance to and fro.

With every twist of a jolly green vine,
The sun makes each fruit feel simply divine.
A chorus of giggles in the warm afternoon,
While the bees drop in, humming a tune.

One lime spills jokes that tickle the pears,
As rib-tickling melodies float on the air.
The oranges wink with a juicy delight,
While the melons just giggle, all through the night.

Each slice tells a story, a funny old jest,
In the orchard of chuckles, we're truly the best.
So come join the fun, let's have a grand spree,
In this merry old garden, so zesty and free!

Citrus Chronicles

Once in a grove where mishaps collide,
A cat tried to dance, then promptly she slide.
The goofy old parrots wrote novels in gold,
Of the legendary citrus, where stories unfold.

Each lemon wore glasses, quite hipster in style,
They chattered away, with a sass and a smile.
A grapefruit with dreams of the big Broadway show,
Sang tunes to the sun, with a fabulous glow.

The limes spread gossip that made others grin,
About who played tricks and the silly old sin.
A hammock of oranges swung low in a breeze,
Where fruit had the time to just laugh and tease.

And as twilight descends, the night lights up bright,
With the berries all painted in twinkling delight.
In this funny old grove, where fun never lacks,
Citrus comedians share laughs and relax.

The Orchard's Secret

Underneath the branches, whispers do creep,
Where the fruit-sorcerers hold secrets to keep.
The apples are giggling, "What a sight to see!"
As the lemons concoct a fruit-themed spree.

A secret society just forms when it rains,
With coconuts cracking at all the refrains.
The stars roll their eyes at the shenanigans here,
As the berries throw parties, fueled by good cheer.

Lively debates 'bout the juiciest pear,
And who makes the best lemonade out of flair.
Though they grumble and fuss, it's all in good jest,
For the laugh of the orchard outshines all the rest.

So come round this place, where the laughter won't cease,
In the garden of fruit, they'll offer you peace.
Just don't bring a broom, it's strictly taboo,
In this funny old orchard, the secrets are true!

Sunlit Citrus Dreams

In a field where the sunbeams giggle and play,
The fruit rolls around in a playful ballet.
With lemons in tutus and oranges in hats,
They twirl and they leap, like enchanted acrobats.

In the shade of the branches, secrets reside,
Where every sweet slice has a story inside.
The limes burst with laughter, their jokes are the best,
As they tickle the kumquats, who snicker and jest.

A grapefruit gleams bright, with a wink of delight,
Calling out to the figs for a silly flight.
They hop on the breeze, like a crew from the sea,
In a sailboat of laughter, all wild and free.

As dusk paints the sky and the crickets take flight,
The citrus ensemble plays on through the night.
So gather round close, let your worries all beam,
In the land of the fruit, we preserve our sweet dreams!

Under the Canopy of Yellow

Under the sun, it sways so bright,
Leaves of green, a cheerful sight.
Squirrels dance, the bees do hum,
Oh, the laughs from all who come.

A quirky bird with a crooked beak,
Sings a tune that's quite unique.
Giggling kids toss peels around,
In this yellow haven, joy is found.

Beneath the branches, stories unfold,
Of sticky hands and rinds of gold.
A lizard sneaks, a clownish act,
Chasing shadows, that's a fact.

So raise a glass of lemonade,
To laughter shared in sun and shade.
With every sip and every cheer,
Life's zestful moments, oh so dear.

Aromas of a Summer Garden

In the garden, scents collide,
Zesty whispers pierce the tide.
A gnome with shades, a painted grin,
Cheers for citrus, let the fun begin!

A rabbit hops with such finesse,
Dodging peas in a fuzzy dress.
The sunflowers twist, they shake with glee,
As the melon asks, 'Come dance with me!'

The marigold winks, quite the tease,
While bees buzz by, hearts at ease.
Frogs in suits debate the game,
Who'll win the crown, or just some fame?

When twilight glows, the fireflies rise,
Lighting paths beneath the skies.
In this garden, joy will linger,
With every laugh, sweet citrus stinger.

Tales of Tangy Delights

Once a fruit with a sassy wink,
Adventures popped with each little squeeze.
Finding friends in every bite,
Creating giggles, pure delight!

A jester lime in a party hat,
Cracks jokes with a zesty spat.
The orange rolled, a clownish feat,
Giggling as it bounced down the street.

In a bowl, they join the fun,
Swapping tales till day is done.
With every slice, a burst of cheer,
A citrus fiesta, oh so dear!

So savor life's tangy thrill,
With friends and laughter, hearts to fill.
Let's raise our spoons, salute the night,
In a world where flavors feel so right.

The Shade of Citrus Dreams

In shadows soft, where dreams take flight,
Citrus secrets dance in light.
A giggling gopher, oh what a sight,
Slides down zesty slopes, pure delight!

While oranges plot a playful heist,
A lime's the lookout, rolling dice.
Together they scheme, their laughter loud,
Chasing mischief through the crowd.

The sunshine fades, stars start to peep,
Silly tales woven, they'll never sleep.
With every wink, the night enthralls,
Underneath the citrus brawls.

From fruity dreams, the tales emerge,
Of laughter wild, a sweet surge.
In every slice, there's joy to beam,
Beneath the shade of citrus dreams.

Stardust and Citrus Harmony

In a garden, bright and sweet,
A citrus dance, oh what a treat!
The stars above, they wink and cheer,
While little bugs hum songs we hear.

Zesty dreams on the vine,
Lemonade wishes, oh so fine!
Juggling fruit with such delight,
Giggles echo through the night.

Each pucker brings a silly grin,
With every twist, new fun begins.
The sun dips low, the day's encore,
Beneath the moon, we laugh some more.

With yellow skins, we sing and play,
In citrus joy, we spend the day.
The world's absurd, yet we abide,
In this fruity dream, we take great pride.

The Twisted Tales of Yellow Skins

Once a combo of fruit and zest,
Yellow skins put to the test.
Banana hats and lemon shoes,
A wacky world, we can't refuse.

Sour jokes that never fade,
Citrus puns, oh, how they invade!
We dance around, twirling delights,
Finding humor in all our sights.

Juicy laughter spills from trees,
As we joke and catch the breeze.
Lemons dressed in fancy flair,
Silly hats, everyone must wear!

The yellow skins tell all their tales,
In every laugh, a giggle trails.
Join the fun, don't miss the show,
In this twisted orchard, come and glow!

Citrus Lullabies in the Orchard

Underneath the citrus skies,
Tiny fruits hum lullabies.
With each note, a sparkle flies,
Bringing giggles, sweet surprise.

From fragrant blooms, the tales unfold,
Of playful tricks and pranks retold.
With every chord, so bright and clear,
The silly dreams are always near.

In the orchard, we find our fun,
As lemon-scented jokes are spun.
Dancing shadows, laughter swirls,
A magical place for boys and girls.

So come and sing this joyful tune,
Beneath the laughs of afternoon.
With citrus shades and playful glee,
Life's a song among the tree!

The Joyful Harvest of Yesteryears

Oh, the harvest, what a sight,
With yellow fruits, so bold, so bright!
Each juicy bite, a laugh we share,
Memories bloom, floating in air.

Tales of clumsiness and falls,
As we toss our fruity balls.
The laughter echoes through the glen,
Oh, how we wish to do it again!

With citrus smiles and funny fables,
Creating joy, we spin our labels.
A time machine in every fruit,
Taking us back to fun, so cute.

As golden hues adorn our dreams,
Life's a tapestry of hearty themes.
So raise a cheer, let's feast and play,
In the joyful harvest of yesterday!

Beneath the Tangy Boughs

In the shade where zany critters play,
Citrus dreams whisper, come what may.
A squirrel in sunglasses, lounging so fine,
Chases down a bee for a splash of sunshine.

A jester in green, on a citrus spree,
Flips peels like pancakes, giggles with glee.
An ant in a dance, with rhythm and cheer,
Making lemonade parties, spreading the beer!

In the midst of the laughter, a lime takes the stage,
Dancing so wild, unleashing a rage.
Beneath tangy boughs, mischief's embraced,
Where fruit finds its joy and laughter's displayed.

With citrus confetti, they plan a grand feast,
Where all of their quirks make the joy increase.
Under the sun, with a wink and a smile,
Beneath tangy boughs, they party in style.

Slices of Sunshine

On a plate of joy, bright and so sweet,
Citrus slices gather for a comical feat.
With giggles they tumble, all yellow and round,
Staging a circus, the funniest found.

A grapefruit juggles, while oranges cheer,
Lemons tightrope walk, with no hint of fear.
Limes throw confetti, all zesty and keen,
Creating a scene that's too funny to glean.

In this fruity circus, the laughter is loud,
As berries do cartwheels, drawing a crowd.
Under the sun, in a citrus parade,
They twirl and they leap, hilarity made.

With each slice of sunshine, a spark of delight,
They burst into giggles, from morning till night.
These slices of joy make the world feel so bright,
In a dance of sweet citrus, laughter takes flight.

The Story of Citrus Breezes

In the gentle breeze, a tale unfolds,
Of citrusy mischief and secrets retold.
A mischievous mango, with a hat of spun gold,
Shares jokes with the lemons, both brave and bold.

With each breeze that blows, a giggle is passed,
As oranges twirl, making good times last.
A grapefruit grins, with a wink from behind,
While every sweet lemon is laughing, not blind.

In the heart of the grove, the fun never ends,
As breezes carry whispers of fruit-loving friends.
They swing from the branches, their laughter will fly,
As the sun dips low, painting the sky.

These are the tales spun in citrus delight,
Where breezes of laughter chase shadows from sight.
In every sweet moment, where humor is bright,
The story goes on through day and through night.

A Grove of Echoes

In a grove full of giggles, echoes abound,
Where citrusy whispers create joyful sound.
A lemon with charm cracks a zesty new joke,
Causing the limes to burst out and choke.

With each silly jest, a new fruit joins in,
A babbling orange, with a grin on its skin.
The cherries chime in, with merry delight,
Creating a symphony, humorous and bright.

As the breeze carries laughter, it paints through the trees,
Where every bright fruit sways with such ease.
In the land of the echoes, the fun never ceases,
As each fruit finds its rhythm, and laughter releases.

Through the grove of echoes, where joy intertwines,
Citrus laughter resonates, crossing sweet lines.
With each silly moment, the past softly glows,
In a grove of such echoes, where happiness flows.

Grappling with Shadows in the Orchard

In the orchard where shadows play,
A pear tried to dance, but fell on the hay.
An apple snickered, it turned to a gourd,
While oranges laughed, their juice they poured.

The scarecrow sighed, what a sight to see,
Chasing squirrels, oh what a spree!
A rabbit hopped by, with a grin so wide,
"Do you need a hat?" it cheekily cried.

The wind swirled and tossed little dreams,
As peaches debated the best of their schemes.
"Let's throw a party!" yelled one with zest,
And all of the fruits felt thoroughly blessed.

Yet one lemon glared, it said, "Not cool!"
"A fruit salad party? You're all such fools!"
They giggled and wiggled, under the tree,
In their citrus world, joyful and free.

Awakening the Borrowed Spring

In cozy corners, a bloom did peak,
While winter whispered, filled with mystique.
A wandering breeze with laughter in tow,
Awoke little buds, giving quite a show.

The daffodils danced, the tulips joined in,
With a jester's cap, oh where to begin?
"Who borrowed spring?" the daisies did fret,
"Let's write a letter; we'll not forget!"

Bumblebees buzzed with jokes in their flight,
As the morning sun rose, so warm and bright.
"Why did the flower go to school?" it asked,
"To improve its petals!" while others just laughed.

So petals rejoiced under skies so blue,
While rascally winds made trouble for two.
Yet every bloom wore a smile with glee,
For in borrowed spring, life danced, carefree.

Citrus and the Celestial

Under starlit skies, a tangerine rolled,
It whispered to oranges, "Do you feel bold?"
With laughter and twinkles, they danced on a beam,
While grapefruit pondered, "Am I part of the team?"

A comet zipped by, trailing zest in its wake,
Carrying secrets that it chose not to shake.
"Why are we saucy?" a lime did exclaim,
"Because we're fruits! We've got quite the fame!"

The moonlight grinned, and the stars chimed in,
With jokes from the cosmos that made their heads spin.
"Why did the stars all come to our jam?"
"Because in their world, we're the fruitiest fam!"

So they twirled and whirled in a cosmic dance,
With planets amused by each citrus chance.
In the hush of space, while laughter took flight,
Citrus fruits sparkled, a whimsical night.

Toast to the Sunshine Peel

A toast to the peel that glimmers so bright,
In their zesty kingdom, a marvelous sight.
"Raise your glasses high!" the bananas did shout,
"For we're the zingers, without a doubt!"

Pineapples swayed with crowns on their heads,
While berries joked stories from their cozy beds.
"Why did the fig join a circus parade?"
"To juggle the sunshine and never get frayed!"

With wigs made of leaves and laughter so loud,
The fruits gathered closely, forming a crowd.
"May our jokes be as sweet as the juice that we share,
And may all our troubles just vanish in air!"

So cheers to the peel, to the shine and the fun,
The orchard together, all basking in sun.
With raucous good humor and zest in their cheer,
Citrus delights, year after year!

The Art of Zesty Reflections

In a world of citrus dreams,
The laughter bursts like sunny beams.
A yellow hue, a squashy grin,
Life's quirks await, let's dive right in.

With every slice, a joy revealed,
In our laughter, the zest is sealed.
Juicy tales of tangy delight,
We giggle as we take a bite.

Puns like peels, so fresh and bright,
Rolling in wit, it feels just right.
The comedy in every squeeze,
As we share our thoughts with ease.

In the orchard, we dare to play,
With zesty jokes to light the way.
Chasing the sun till twilight's close,
In citrus scents, our laughter grows.

Golden Fruits and Silver Memories

Oh golden orbs upon the vine,
Each one a treasure, so divine.
We dance around with glee anew,
As memories sprinkle morning dew.

With every bite, a smile is found,
Unexpected laughter all around.
Juicy secrets, tales unfold,
Like silver stars, their warmth we hold.

Ridiculous quirks, our hearts align,
With silhouettes that paint the line.
The fruit parade, a jester's show,
Each twist and turn, a playful flow.

In laughter's embrace, we all confide,
A citrus patch where joys collide.
So grab a slice, let's make a toast,
To golden moments we love the most.

Halos of Yellow in Evening Glow

As twilight wraps the day in gold,
In citrus worlds, we dare be bold.
Giggles linger in the air,
Under halos, we dance without a care.

My quirky friends with traits so fine,
A lemon twist on life's design.
Each joke is ripe, the punchlines swell,
In laughter's grip, we weave our spell.

With zesty tales that hit the mark,
We find the humor in the spark.
Yellow visions in our sights,
Chasing shadows until the night.

In the twilight's warm embrace we share,
Our fruity jokes beyond compare.
With zest as fuel and fun as creed,
In every heart, a citrus seed.

Citrus Sunbeams and Moonlit Tales

Under sunbeams, laughter flows,
With zesty tales, anything goes.
In every citrus, joy does thrive,
Where funny thoughts come so alive.

Moonlit gatherings, winks and grins,
We trade our stories, where laughter wins.
In the glow, we squeeze the night,
Expressing joy, our spirits bright.

The citrus dance, a quirky sight,
As jokes collide in sheer delight.
With every pucker, we share our glee,
Oh what a zany jubilee!

So raise a glass to all who smile,
In citrus worlds, we go the extra mile.
With sun and moon as our guides,
In zesty joy, our friendship resides.

The Orchard's Embrace

In a garden where laughter hides,
Citizens of citrus wear silly strides.
With every twist and every puckered grin,
The fruit dances, and chaos begins.

Pies fly high like dreams in flight,
While squirrels plot beneath the twilight.
Frogs croak tunes of juicy delight,
Who knew orchards could spark such a sight?

Lemon drops roll like marbles lost,
While blossoms giggle, counting the cost.
Sunshine giggles at the green leaves' tease,
Nature's jesters, forever at ease.

Yet in this haven, joy's the decree,
Where fruit's mischief sets worries free.
Under the branches, laughter does swell,
In this quirky orchard, all is well.

Pudding the Past with Pith

In a kitchen where chaos reigns,
Pudding is flopping like runaway trains.
Citrus zest flies like stars at night,
While family debates what's truly right.

Grandpa swears he knows the best pie,
But his recipe's lost, oh my, oh my!
With oranges juggling and lemons in tow,
They concoct a mess that continues to grow!

Mom's on a mission; she's whisking with flair,
To create a surprise with citrus in air.
But the pith tells tales of yesteryear's food,
Leaving everyone puzzled, just slightly crude.

They laugh at the past, each bite paving way,
To pudding nostalgia — it brightens the gray.
In this citrus circus, joy's never late,
Even when cake turns a tad out of date.

Nectar of Tomorrow

Beneath the sky, a sweet nectar flows,
Where bees wear sunglasses and humor glows.
They buzz on a mission, taking it slow,
Preparing for tomorrow, putting on a show.

With flowers winking at the bumblebee,
And oranges gossiping, oh can't you see?
They dip in the sun and roll in delight,
Creating tomorrow from today's crazy flight.

Dandelions dance with the wind so spry,
While fruit tells tales with a cheeky sigh.
A picnic brigade, they line up in rows,
Eyes twinkling like stars where the sweetness glows.

So let's raise a toast with a fizzy cheer,
To citrus dreams and futures so clear!
In this vibrant hive, joy's the decree,
Crafting sweet nectar, wild and carefree.

Citrus of Today

The sun shines bright on this radiant day,
Where citrus laughter leads the way.
A zesty crew of colors begins to play,
As giggles escape, come what may.

Lemons dressed in polka dots stand tall,
While others pile up for a limbo ball.
Limes roll by with stories untold,
In this comedy fest, so bold and gold.

A grapefruit juggles, oh what a sight!
As oranges cheer for the ultimate flight.
Bouncing and bouncing beneath a sunbeam,
In this citrus world, laughter's the theme.

So here's to the fruit, both zesty and bright,
Creating joy with wondrous delight.
With each playful moment, sweet journeys pave,
In this orchard of laughs, forever we rave.

Vibrance in Every Sunlit Fruit

In gardens where giggles mingle with sun,
Each fruit's a character full of fun.
A tangerine topsy-turvy in cheer,
With a sly little smile, it winks from the sphere.

Bananas gather, wearing silly hats,
Chasing their friends, racing agile chats.
The pomegranates cheer, rolling down hills,
With juicy joy that's bringing the thrills.

Under the branches, mischief runs free,
With each heartfelt chuckle, we dance with glee.
A game of fruit tag begins in a flash,
With each vibrant belly laugh leading the dash.

So here's to the moments where sunlight plays,
Making merriment in the brightest of rays.
In every sweet bite, there's fun to embrace,
In this fruit-filled kingdom, we find our place.

www.ingramcontent.com/pod-product-compliance
Lightning Source LLC
Chambersburg PA
CBHW070309120526
44590CB00017B/2600